WHOLE HEARTED

A DAILY DEVOTIONAL TO HELP YOU
BECOME A WHOLEHEARTED
FOLLOWER OF JESUS

KEVIN ELOY

WHOLEHEARTED: Daily Devotionals to Help You Become a Wholehearted Follower of Jesus

Copyright © 2025 by Kevin Eloy

For more about this author, please visit https://www.kevineloy.com/

All rights reserved. No part of this publication may be reproduced, distributed, or transmitted in any form or by any means, including photocopying, recording, or other electronic or mechanical methods, without the prior written permission of the author, except in the case of brief quotations embodied in critical reviews and certain other noncommercial uses permitted by copyright law.

No part of this book may be used for the training of artificial systems, including systems based on artificial intelligence (AI), without the copyright owner's prior permission. This prohibition shall be in force even on platforms and systems that claim to have such rights based on an implied contract for hosting the book.

Library of Congress Control Number: 2025903385

Paperback ISBN: 978-1-966283-04-1
Hardcover ISBN: 978-1-966283-07-2

1. Main category—Religion & Spirituality › Christian Books & Bibles › Worship & Devotion › Devotionals
2. Other category—Nonfiction › Self-Help › Spiritual
3. Other category—Religion & Spirituality › Christian Books & Bibles › Christian Living › Spiritual Growth

Published by: AR PRESS
Roger L. Brooks, Publisher
roger@americanrealpublishing.com
americanrealpublishing.com

DO NOT GIVE UP
You May Be Closer Than You Think

This was the first devotional I ever wrote for the channel, and in some ways, it's still my favorite. I thought it only right to start the book with it also.

This is the story of Florence Chadwick.

Florence was an accomplished swimmer, the first woman to swim the English Channel both ways. In 1952, she set out to do something even more challenging—swim the twenty-six-mile stretch from the California coast to Catalina Island. After fifteen grueling hours, a thick fog rolled in, surrounding her and obscuring her vision. She couldn't see where she was or how far she had left to go.

Exhausted and discouraged, Florence wanted nothing more than to quit. The fog had disoriented her, and her body and mind were drained. Despite her support team in the boat urging her to keep going, she couldn't take it any longer. She climbed into the boat, defeated, only to discover she was less than half a mile from shore. She was *so close* but couldn't see it because of the fog.

Just like Florence, we can sometimes find ourselves in a fog of exhaustion, discouragement, or confusion. It can feel like the end is nowhere in sight, and quitting may seem like the best option. But here's what I want to tell you:

YOU MAY BE CLOSER THAN YOU THINK.

Galatians 6:9 (NIV) reminds us,

"Let us not become weary in doing good, for at the proper time we will reap a harvest if we do not give up."

DON'T GIVE UP—KEEP MOVING FORWARD

When you feel like giving up, remember that the breakthrough could be just around the corner. You might not be able to see it yet, but it's there.

If you've been tempted to quit—whether it's in your faith, your marriage, your career, or a personal battle—I'm here to encourage you to pick up that towel, wipe the sweat off your brow, and keep moving forward.

Just like Florence, you might be closer to your goal than you realize. The fog will lift, and you'll see how far you've come.

CONCLUSION

God is faithful, and He promises that in due time, if we keep pressing on, we will reap the reward. So today, even if you feel exhausted, disoriented, or ready to quit, keep going. You're closer than you think.

_____

_____

_____

_____

_____

_____

WHY DO BAD THINGS HAPPEN TO GOOD PEOPLE?
The Real Answer May Shock You…

Now, here's where I might step on some toes.

We often ask, "Why do bad things happen to *good* people?" But here's the truth: None of us are good.

The Bible says, "All have sinned and fall short of the glory of God." (Romans 3:23, NIV) Jesus is the only one who was truly good—the only perfect person. The only time something truly bad happened to someone good was to Jesus, and He volunteered for it.

JESUS'S SACRIFICE IS THE ULTIMATE EXAMPLE OF SUFFERING

God didn't sit in heaven untouched by our pain. He entered into it. Jesus, the Son of God, left the glory of heaven to come to earth. He was born into poverty, lived a humble life, and was mocked as an illegitimate child. He was rejected by His own family, abandoned by His friends, falsely accused, and wrongfully imprisoned.

Jesus endured the ultimate suffering when he was beaten, tortured, and nailed to a cross, hanging in shame. But the worst part wasn't the physical pain. On the cross, Jesus *became sin* for us, and for the first time, He was separated from His Father. He experienced a kind of pain and abandonment we'll never fully understand. God allowed this so that Jesus could suffer *with* us and *for* us.

SO WHY DOES GOD ALLOW SUFFERING?

I won't pretend to have all the answers for every situation. But here's what I do know: The reason for suffering is *not* that God doesn't love us.

John 3:16 (NIV) reminds us, "For God so loved the world that He gave His one and only Son, that whoever believes in Him shall not perish but have eternal life." God's love is so immense that He was willing to let His Son endure the worst suffering imaginable.

GOD'S LOVE IN OUR PAIN

God loves us so much that He took our pain and suffering seriously—seriously enough to let Jesus bear it. When we go through hardship, we're not alone. We have a Savior who understands because He's been there. He came into our broken world and shared in our suffering, all because of His love for us.

The question of why bad things happen may not always have a direct answer, but what we can know for sure is this: God loves us deeply, and through Jesus's suffering, He made a way to bring us back to Him.

CONCLUSION

When we ask, "Why do bad things happen to good people?" we should remember that Jesus, the only truly good person, endured the ultimate suffering so we could be redeemed. And through His pain, we can find hope, peace, and the assurance that God loves us more than we could ever imagine.

BE ON GUARD

Have You Ever Given in to Temptation and Regretted It?

Scripture: "Be on your guard; stand firm in the faith; be courageous; be strong."
(1 Corinthians 16:13, NIV)

Chances are, you didn't plan to give in to temptation. You didn't wake up one day thinking, *Today, I'm going to wreck my life*. No one plans to end up forty pounds overweight, file for bankruptcy, or destroy their marriage through lies and deception. But the problem is that many people also don't plan *not* to.

WHY DO WE FALL?

We often fall into temptation simply because we're not ready. Jesus Himself warned us about this when He said, "Watch and pray so that you will not fall into temptation. The spirit is willing, but the flesh is weak."
(Matthew 26:41)

How many times have you found yourself giving in to something you later regretted? Why? Because you weren't on your guard. You weren't prepared. Temptation has a way of sneaking up on us, and if we're not ready, we fall into its trap.

WHY SHOULD WE BE ON OUR GUARD?
The Devil Is Coming for You

The Bible tells us Satan's mission is to steal, kill, and destroy. (John 10:10, NIV) In 2 Corinthians 2:11 (NLT), Paul warns the church, "so that Satan will not outsmart us. For we are familiar with his evil schemes."

The devil has schemes, and he's targeting you. He wants to ruin your life, destroy your relationships, and take away your peace. That's why it's essential to be on your guard.

But here's the good news:
You aren't fighting in your own power.

You are fighting with Christ's power—not *for* victory, but *from* victory. Because of Jesus's death and resurrection, we already have miraculous authority over the darkness in His name. We aren't struggling in a losing battle; we're standing in a victory that has already been won.

STAND FIRM IN CHRIST'S POWER

The key to resisting temptation is to stand firm in Christ. On your own, your flesh is weak. But with Jesus, you have strength, courage, and power. Paul's encouragement to "be on your guard, stand firm in the faith, be courageous, and be strong" is not just a call to action—it's a reminder that when you rely on God's strength, you are equipped with everything you need to fight temptation.

CONCLUSION

Today, don't just go through the motions of life. Be on your guard. The devil has a plan to derail your faith, but God has already given you the tools to stand firm. Watch, pray, and prepare yourself with Christ's power. You don't have to fall into temptation—you can overcome it, not by your strength, but by His.

STOP TRYING TO FIND YOUR PURPOSE

The Greatest Tragedy in Life Is Not Death, but a Life Without Purpose

We've all asked the question, "What's my purpose?" It's a question many people spend their lives trying to answer. Yes, God has a purpose for you, but it's not about you.

Here are three quick principles of purpose that can help guide you toward the life God has called you to live:

1. YOUR PURPOSE ISN'T FOR YOU—YOUR PURPOSE IS GOD'S PURPOSE

So often, we focus on finding "our" purpose, as if it's something hidden or elusive, but the truth is, your purpose is not about you. It's about fulfilling *God's* purpose for your life. We were created to glorify God and serve His kingdom. When you align yourself with His will, you will find the true meaning of your life.

2. YOU DON'T *FIND* YOUR PURPOSE, YOU *SERVE* GOD'S PURPOSE

When David was out in the field as a shepherd, he wasn't seeking a position—he was serving a purpose. David wasn't trying to become famous or find his "big break."

When Goliath was taunting the Israelites and the whole army was afraid, God didn't choose David because he was the most ripped warrior or because he had the most influence. David wasn't a rich, powerful leader with thousands of followers on social media. He was just a young boy, faithfully delivering lunch to his brothers on the battlefield.

David wasn't hoping for his moment of glory—he was simply "serving where God had placed him." His heart was focused on obedience, not on seeking a platform.

3. TO SERVE GOD'S PURPOSE, START SERVING GOD'S PEOPLE

God's purpose isn't about chasing platforms, positions, or power. It's about serving people. If you're not sure what your purpose is, start by serving others. Don't let the enemy rob you of your "why" by making you focus on the wrong things. David was a man after God's own heart, and that's why he served God's purpose.

Are you feeling lost or unsure of your purpose? Begin by serving others, and you'll find that God's purpose for your life will unfold naturally. As you humble yourself and focus on the needs of others, you will see how God uses your service to fulfill His greater plan.

STOP SEARCHING FOR YOUR OWN GLORY

The purest definition of sin (from the Greek word *hamartia*) is "missing the mark," and that includes missing God's purpose for your life. When we live life apart from God's purpose, it leads to confusion, emptiness, and despair. We end up treating life like an experiment, constantly searching for meaning through different jobs, relationships, vacations, or experiences. We've unintentionally reduced our lives to a string of self-focused attempts to "find ourselves."

We often hear messages like "find yourself," "treat yourself," and "do you." But the result? We see people who are popular but miserable, powerful but unsatisfied, prosperous but depressed. Why? Because they are searching for something in this world that the world can't provide.

WE WERE CREATED FOR HEAVEN, NOT FOR THIS WORLD

You weren't made for this world—you were made for heaven. Yet we spend so much of our lives searching for purpose in temporary things, hoping they will bring us eternal satisfaction. But the truth is, nothing in this world can satisfy the longing in our hearts that only God can fill. When we chase after the things of this world, we miss out on the eternal joy and fulfillment that comes from knowing and serving God.

CONCLUSION

If you're wondering what your purpose is, start serving God's people today. Stop seeking personal glory and start seeking God's heart. As you do, you'll discover God's purpose for your life isn't something you find—it's something you live out every day.

_____

_____

_____

_____

_____

_____

_____

_____

_____

GOD IS HOLY
Who Is God?

God's holiness may not be the most popular topic, but it is one of the most mentioned in the Bible, appearing 637 times. If you truly experience the holiness of God, it will shake you, stir you, and bring you to your knees in repentance, causing you to fall on your face in worship.

THE VISION OF ISAIAH

In Isaiah 6, we see a profound image of God's holiness. The prophet Isaiah received this vision in the year King Uzziah died—a king who had reigned for fifty-two years, starting at the young age of sixteen. His death left the people anxious and unsettled. But in this uncertain time, Isaiah saw the Lord, high and exalted, seated on a throne, and the train of His robe filled the temple.

Above the Lord were the seraphim—angelic beings with six wings, worshipping the Almighty. Their voices shook the temple, which was filled with smoke. The seraphim, with their six wings, used:

- Two wings to fly.
- Two wings to cover their faces, to shield themselves from the overwhelming glory of God.
- Two wings to cover their feet, as they stood near holy ground.

And as they flew, they cried out in Hebrew, *"Kadosh, kadosh, kadosh,"* which means *Holy, holy, holy.*

HOLY, HOLY, HOLY

In Hebrew, repeating a word emphasizes its importance. Jesus did this when He said, "Verily, verily" to underscore the truth of His words. But of all of God's attributes, *holiness* is the only one repeated three times in a row. You never hear "Mercy, mercy, mercy" or "Love, love, love." It's "Holy, holy, holy"—a declaration of God's ultimate nature.

WHAT IS HOLINESS?

In our culture, the word *holy* gets thrown around in various contexts—Holy Communion, holy matrimony, the Holy Ghost, the Holy Grail, and even phrases like "holy cow" or "holy smoke." But true holiness means something far more profound. It means to be *separate, set apart, a cut above*.

Tony Evans uses the analogy of special dishes. Some are everyday dishes from Walmart or Target, but others are the fine china, set apart for special occasions.

God's holiness is a cut above everything else. He is *completely and entirely holy*. God is all-good, all-pure, all-righteous, and all-perfect, without fault or blemish. He is infinite, immutable, immeasurable, and incomprehensible.

GOD IS SELF-SUFFICIENT

God's holiness also means He is self-existent, self-sustaining, and self-sufficient. Consider this:

- God has wisdom He didn't need to learn.
- God has strength He didn't need to earn.
- God has love He didn't need to receive to know how to give.

God is the One who was, who is, and who is to come. There is no one like our God—He is set apart from everything and everyone.

CONCLUSION

Take a moment today to reflect on the holiness of God. He is not just a little bit better or a little bit wiser—He is completely other. He is above all, and there is nothing in this world that can compare to Him. Stand in awe of His holiness and worship Him, for there is truly no one like our God.

STOP BEING OFFENDED

Have You Noticed How Easily People Are Offended These Days?

It seems like people today are quick to take offense—Christians included. Some might even think that as followers of Jesus, it's part of our job to be offended.

After all, shouldn't we point out sins, criticize the culture, and take a bold stand for truth? Shouldn't we get upset about all the injustices and sins we see around us? (#BeingSarcastic)

But is that really what we're called to do?

Let's look at what Scripture says.

QUICK TO LISTEN, SLOW TO SPEAK, SLOW TO BECOME ANGRY

The Bible gives clear guidance on how we should respond to the world around us. In James 1:19 (NIV), it says, "Everyone should be quick to listen, slow to speak and slow to become angry."

How well are you doing with that?

Think about how Jesus handled situations. He was asked 183 questions during His ministry and directly answered only three of them. In fact, He asked more questions—307, to be exact. This shows us Jesus wasn't quick to anger or eager to defend Himself. He listened more than He spoke and modeled patience.

WHAT OFFENDS YOU?

We've all been there—getting upset over the little things. Someone cuts us off in traffic, doesn't respond to our text message right away, or takes a call during a movie. Our anger can flare up quickly, but it's usually over minor annoyances.

If we're being honest, some of us actually *like* being angry. We don't enjoy what made us mad, but we enjoy the feeling of being upset. Why? Because when we're angry, we feel morally superior.

We feel justified in our anger, as if being offended somehow makes us better or more righteous than the person who wronged us.

YOUR ANGER DOESN'T LEAD TO RIGHTEOUSNESS

But here's a sobering truth: "Your human anger does not produce the righteousness that God desires." (James 1:20) Getting offended doesn't make you more righteous, nor does it draw you closer to God. In fact, it often pulls us further away from what really matters—loving others the way Jesus loved us.

JESUS DIDN'T CALL US TO BE RIGHT—HE CALLED US TO BE LOVING

Jesus didn't come to win arguments. He came to win hearts. He didn't call us to be right all the time; yet He called us to be loving. Our goal as Christians isn't to make a point, but it's to make a difference. And the way we do that is by being "quick to listen, slow to speak, and slow to become angry."

CONCLUSION
Make a Difference, Not Just a Point

It's time to stop being so easily offended. The next time you feel anger rising up, ask yourself if it's worth it. Does your offense reflect the love of Jesus? Is your anger helping anyone or just making you feel self-righteous?

Instead of being quick to anger, let's commit to being quick to listen and slow to speak. Let's be less concerned about proving ourselves right and more focused on being loving, compassionate, and understanding. After all, that's the way of Jesus.

THERE'S PURPOSE IN YOUR PAIN

People Don't Hate Pain— We Hate Pain Without Purpose!

When bad things happen—like a car wreck, a spouse cheating, a breakup, losing a job, or battling cancer—one of the first questions we often ask is, "Why is this happening?" We cry out to God, "Where are You?" We wonder why life seems unfair, especially when we've been trying to do everything right—read our Bible, go to church, help others. It feels unjust, and we desperately search for a purpose in our suffering.

The truth is, people don't hate pain itself—they hate pain without a reason. But when there is purpose, we can endure so much more than we ever imagined.

PAIN WITH PURPOSE

Here's a powerful reality: People can endure a lot of pain if they know there is purpose behind it.

- Some people will endure the pain of running a marathon because of the satisfaction they feel at the finish line.

- Others will go through the intense pain of withdrawal because they know it will lead to the freedom of sobriety.

- Childbirth is incredibly painful, but mothers endure it for the joy of bringing new life into the world.

SOMETIMES, GOD'S PREPARATION COMES PACKAGED AS PAIN

Rather than just seeing life through the lens of your pain, try to see your pain through the lens of God's purpose.

GOD'S PURPOSE IN ALL THINGS

Romans 8:28 (NIV) reminds us of this truth:

> "And we know that in all things God works for the good of those who love him, who have been called according to his purpose."

Notice that it doesn't say God works *some* things for good—it says *all things*. God works *in everything*, even in our pain, to bring about His purpose. That doesn't mean the pain itself is good, but God can use it for good.

Your suffering is not in vain. There is a purpose, even when you can't see it. God is at work in ways you may not understand right now, but He is using it to shape you, prepare you, and strengthen you for what He has in store.

CONCLUSION

One thing is certain—God never wastes a hurt. He can use your pain, your hurt, your fear, and your uncertainty to bring about good. Your pain can become the very thing that equips you to help someone else who's going through a similar trial.

Trust that God is working even in the most painful moments. There's purpose in your pain. Let Him use it for His glory and your good.

_____

_____

_____

_____

GOD STILL SPEAKS

God Is Always Speaking—The Real Question Is, Are You Listening?

We often rush through life consumed by noise, distractions, and busyness. But if we want to hear God's voice, we need to learn how to listen. So, how do we learn to hear God's voice?

BE STILL

The first step to hearing God's voice is to learn to *be still*. Psalm 46:10 (NIV) tells us exactly how to experience God's presence: "Be still, and know that I am God."

Notice what God *doesn't* say—He doesn't say, "Be frantic," or "Be busy." He doesn't tell us to seek Him on the go, while rushing from one thing to the next. He tells us to be still.

To hear God, we need to slow down, quiet our minds, and turn down the noise of the world. But how does God speak?

HOW DOES GOD SPEAK?
1. GOD SPEAKS THROUGH HIS WORD

The primary way God speaks to us is through Scripture. His Word directs, guides, and corrects us. Hebrews 4:12 reminds us God's Word is alive and active. It speaks to us with the same power today as it did thousands of years ago.

2. GOD SPEAKS THROUGH PEOPLE

Sometimes, God uses others to deliver His message. A godly friend, a family member, or a sermon can be the very vessel God uses to get your attention. How many times has someone spoken a word of wisdom or encouragement right when you needed it?

3. GOD SPEAKS THROUGH CIRCUMSTANCES

God often speaks to us through the situations we face—both the doors He opens and the doors He closes. We might get frustrated when things don't go the way we planned, but God can speak even through a closed door. Have you ever thanked God for the door He closed? For the relationship that didn't work out?

4. GOD SPEAKS THROUGH HIS SPIRIT

God also speaks through the Holy Spirit, prompting, moving, and leading us. You may feel a nudge in your heart, an overwhelming peace about a decision, or a conviction you can't ignore.

BE READY FOR WHAT HE SAYS

Here's the thing: Don't ask God to speak if you don't want to hear what He has to say. Sometimes what God says may convict you, challenge you, or stretch you beyond your comfort zone. It might even scare you because it feels impossible. But that's how you know it's God—He often calls us to things bigger than ourselves, things that require faith and dependence on Him.

CONCLUSION

God is speaking. The question is, are you listening? Slow down, be still, and open your heart to what He is saying. It may not always be comfortable, but it will always be worth it. He is ready to guide, direct, and lead you if you're ready to listen.

HOLY GROUND

Why Take Off Your Shoes on Holy Ground?

Here's a question: Why would God ask someone to take off their shoes when they're standing on holy ground?

There's an old song we used to sing growing up, called "Standing on Holy Ground," and lately, those words have been speaking to me. This idea of holy ground comes from a powerful moment in the Bible, one that we find in Exodus 3.

When God calls Moses from the burning bush, Moses responds, and God says this in verse 5 (NIV): "Do not come any closer. Take off your sandals, for the place where you are standing is holy ground."

WHAT DOES IT MEAN TO TAKE OFF YOUR SHOES?

First off, taking off your shoes is a sign of *respect and reverence.* In most cultures, shoes represent the dirt and grime of the world. We take them off at the door so we don't track in the mess we've been walking through. God was telling Moses, "Leave behind the filth of the world; this place is holy."

But there's more to it. Here's the cool part—in Jewish culture, when you get home, you take off your shoes. You are stepping into a place of belonging, a place of rest. God was telling Moses, "You are home in My presence."

YOU ARE MEANT TO BE HOLY GROUND

When God calls you into His presence, He calls you to something deeper. You're not just on holy ground—you are meant to be holy ground.

Just as God's presence dwelled in the burning bush, He desires to dwell in us. The Bible reminds us of this truth in Acts 17:24 (NIV):

"The God who made the world and everything in it is the Lord of heaven and earth and does not live in temples built by human hands."

Yet, even though He doesn't dwell in temples made by hands, He chooses to reside in us. We are His holy temple.

CONCLUSION

God's presence is home. When you're in God's presence, you are home. It's a place where you don't just visit—you abide. So, just as Moses took off his sandals, may you take off the burdens, sins, and distractions of the world and let the presence of God find a home in your life.

You are standing on holy ground, and you are meant to carry that holiness with you wherever you go.

_____

_____

_____

_____

_____

_____

CALLING COSTS

You Are Called by God to Change Your World

God has a purpose and a calling for your life. You are called—not just to exist, but to make a difference in the world. But here's the thing: The moment you step into your calling, you step out of your comfort zone.

TWO QUALITIES OF CALLING:
1. CALLING COSTS

When God calls you, there will be a price to pay. Take the story of Saul (later known as Paul). When God called him, he was blinded by a bright light. He didn't know what was happening at first, and God didn't explain everything to him immediately. But once Saul's sight was restored, he had a powerful calling on his life.

Here was a man with a crazy strong resume—he had influence, connections, and a massive platform. Yet when God called him, He didn't promise him success or comfort. Instead, God said this to Ananias about Saul:

"But the Lord said to Ananias, 'Go! This man is my chosen instrument to proclaim my name to the Gentiles and their kings and to the people of Israel. I will show him how much he must suffer for my name.'"
—Acts 9:15-16 (NIV)

GOD'S CALLING COMES WITH A COST

You might be God's chosen instrument for a specific purpose, but that doesn't mean the road will be easy. Like Paul, you may face rejection, misunderstanding, and even suffering.

God often uses our deepest pain to launch our greatest calling. Public callings are often fueled by private pain. Serving Jesus is a gift, but it is also a grind. It's a thrill to live out your purpose, but it's also a burden. Ministry can be exhilarating but also exhausting.

2. CALLING REQUIRES SACRIFICE

One of the biggest enemies of your calling is *comfort*. We all want things to be easy, to stay in familiar places. But your calling will demand that you push beyond the comfortable. God never promised that following Him would be easy, but He promised it would be worth it.

Don't let your desire for comfort keep you from walking in your God-given purpose. Never sacrifice your calling on the altar of comfort.

CONCLUSION

If following Jesus is not both the *greatest gift* and the *greatest burden*, you might not be fully stepping into your calling. There is joy in following Him, but it comes with challenges.

Calling costs, but when you embrace it, you change the world.

What has God called you to do? What are you willing to sacrifice to fulfill that calling?

_____

_____

_____

_____

_____

CHOOSE SURRENDER
Stop Trying to Control Everything

We've all been there, trying to control every aspect of life. Whether it's our schedules, finances, relationships, or even the opinions of others, we can often feel the need to manage it all. But here's the hard truth: **Your need to control may reveal your biggest area of spiritual vulnerability.**

Think about it for a moment—what are you trying to control the most? Whatever it is, it's likely where you're trusting God the least.

CONTROL VS. SURRENDER

When we struggle to trust God, we end up trying to control more and more. This leads to a cycle: the less we trust God, the more we try to control, and the more we try to control, the more we fear losing that control. It's exhausting.

But here's the good news: You don't always have the power to control, but you always have the power to surrender.

Jesus didn't invite us into a life of *comfort and ease*. He invited us to live a life of *sacrifice and surrender*. When you follow Jesus, it means letting go of your need to control and trusting Him with everything—your future, your family, your finances, your fears.

WHAT ARE YOU TRYING TO CONTROL?

Take a moment and ask yourself: *What am I trying to control that God is asking me to surrender?*

Maybe it's your career path, your children's future, or even the fear of the unknown. Whatever it is, God is calling you to release that grip and trust Him fully.

CONCLUSION

Cast your cares on him. God doesn't want you to carry the burden of control and anxiety. "Cast all your cares on Him because He cares for you."
(1 Peter 5:7, RGT)

Let go of the weight you're carrying. Surrender it to God, knowing He is able to handle what you cannot.

So today, choose surrender over control. Trust that God's plan is better, His ways are higher, and His love is enough.
Let go, and let God lead.

_____

_____

_____

_____

_____

_____

_____

_____

_____

_____

FIGHT THE DRIFT
Does God Feel Far Away?

Have you ever been at the beach, playing in the water, and suddenly realized you've drifted far from where you started? The currents can pull you away without you even noticing. Life with God can feel the same way—drifting happens gradually, but before you know it, you feel distant from Him.

Hebrews 2:1 (NIV) warns us: "We must pay more careful attention, therefore, to what we have heard, so that we do not drift away."

The drift doesn't require effort. It's easy to slowly slip away if we're not intentional about staying close to God.

FOUR WAYS TO FIGHT THE DRIFT:
1. SPEND TIME WITH GOD

This seems obvious, but it's vital. How can we expect to feel close to God when we aren't intentional about spending time with Him?

Make it a priority to read the Bible, pray, worship, and attend church. But don't just attend—engage! Get involved, serve, and seek community. Staying close to God requires a daily investment of time and focus.

2. HANG AROUND GODLY PEOPLE

It's impossible to live the right life if you're surrounded by the wrong people. Scripture reminds us in 1 Corinthians 15:33 (NIV), "Do not be misled: 'Bad company corrupts good character.'"

Make sure the people you spend time with are encouraging you to grow closer to God, not leading you away from Him. Surround yourself with those who challenge you in your faith.

3. FIGHT TEMPTATION

James 1:14-15 (NIV) explains the cycle of temptation: "Each person is tempted when they are dragged away by their own evil desire and enticed. Then, after desire has conceived, it gives birth to sin; and sin, when it is full-grown, gives birth to death."

Temptation can drag you further from God if you don't confront it. Don't rationalize your sin or hide it. Ask God for forgiveness and seek the strength to resist the things pulling you away.

The reality is that sin will take you farther than you want to go, keep you longer than you want to stay, and cost you more than you want to pay.

4. DO NOT LOVE THIS WORLD

1 John 2:15 (NIV) says,
"Do not love the world or anything in the world. If anyone loves the world, love for the Father is not in them."

This world is not your home, so don't get caught up in its materialism and temporary pleasures. Fix your eyes on eternal things and remember God hasn't moved—you may have drifted, but He's always right there, waiting for you to return.

CONCLUSION

God has not moved. If God feels far away, take a moment to ask yourself: *Have I drifted?* He is always near, but we must make the intentional choice to stay close to Him. Fight the drift, lean into His presence, and you'll find He is right there with you, every step of the way.

WAITING ON GOD
Waiting Stinks!

Let's be real—waiting can be one of the most frustrating things in life. We hate waiting for water to boil, sitting in traffic, or being stuck in airport delays. But there are bigger things we wait for too: waiting to conceive, waiting to get married, waiting on a prodigal child to come home, waiting for a job opportunity, waiting for healing, or waiting for someone to come to Christ.

We've all been there—praying, believing, and waiting. But why does it seem like God isn't doing anything? Why doesn't He just step in and fix the situation?

KEY TRUTH: WITH GOD, A WAITING SEASON IS NEVER A WASTED SEASON

Let's look at John 11, the story of Mary, Martha, and their brother Lazarus. They were good friends of Jesus's. Lazarus got sick, and they immediately sent word to Jesus, expecting Him to come right away.

"Lord, the one you love is sick." (John 11:3, NIV)

But Jesus didn't come immediately. Hour after hour, they waited. It seemed like God was delaying, and they were left wondering why. Yet, there are two crucial lessons to remember when waiting on God.

1. GOD'S DELAYS ARE NOT NECESSARILY GOD'S DENIALS

In verse 4, Jesus says something profound: "This sickness will not end in death. No, it is for God's glory so that God's Son may be glorified through it."
(John 11:4, NIV)

Mary and Martha didn't know this, but Jesus was planning something far greater than they could imagine. Just because there's a delay, doesn't mean God isn't working.

Many delays are divine delays, where God wants to accomplish something in you before He does something for you. Even when you don't see anything happening, God is working behind the scenes.

By the time Jesus arrived, Lazarus had been dead for four days. In fact, the body had started to decay—it "stinketh," as the King James Version says in John 11:17. All hope seemed lost, but this brings us to the next key lesson.

2. IF GOD ALWAYS MET YOUR EXPECTATIONS, HE'D NEVER HAVE THE OPPORTUNITY TO EXCEED THEM

Mary and Martha wanted a healing, but Jesus had something far greater in mind: a resurrection.

Jesus told Martha, "I am the resurrection and the life. The one who believes in me will live, even though they die." (John 11:25, NIV)

Jesus essentially told her, "I am not just able to resurrect. I am the resurrection." What they saw as the end of the story was really just the beginning of an incredible miracle.

THE SCENE OF YOUR GREATEST DISAPPOINTMENT MAY BE THE SETTING OF YOUR GREATEST MIRACLE.

Sometimes, what we're waiting for doesn't happen the way we expect. But God's plans are always higher than ours, and His timing is always perfect.

CONCLUSION

Trust God's timing. If it's not God's time, you can't force it. But when it is God's time, nothing can stop it! So in your waiting, remember God's delays are not denials. He may be setting you up for something far greater than you've ever imagined.

Keep trusting, keep believing, and know that your waiting season is not a wasted season.

TAKE EVERY THOUGHT CAPTIVE

Most of Life's Battles Are Won or Lost in Your Mind

We have a spiritual enemy who constantly works to shape our thinking, one thought at a time. If we're not careful, we may end up *living* in a prison of lies, believing things about ourselves and God that simply aren't true.

But here's the good news:
God's Word has the power to not only help us but to *transform* us. It can renew our minds with *truth*.

THE BATTLE OF THE MIND

2 Corinthians 10:3-5 (NIV) reminds us:

"For though we live in the world, we do not wage war as the world does. The weapons we fight with are not the weapons of the world. On the contrary, they have divine power to demolish strongholds. We demolish arguments and every pretension that sets itself up against the knowledge of God, and we take captive every thought to make it obedient to Christ."

WHAT ARE THE STRONGHOLDS HOLDING YOU BACK?

We all have strongholds—lies the enemy plants in our minds that keep us from living in freedom. The first step to freedom is to *name* the stronghold. Why?

BECAUSE YOU CAN'T DEFEAT WHAT YOU CAN'T DEFINE.

Maybe your stronghold sounds like:

- I'm not good enough.
- My past is too bad to overcome.
- I'll always struggle with this.
- I'll never be close to God.
- All my relationships end in failure.

CAPTURING AND REPLACING THE LIES

Once you've identified the lie, the next step is to capture it and replace it with God's truth. God has given us His Word as our offensive weapon
—the sword of the Spirit.

Here are some examples of replacing lies with truth:

Lie: "I can't get it all done."

Truth: "I can do all things through Christ who strengthens me." (Phil 4:13, NKJV)

Lie: "I'm not attractive; I don't like the way I look."

Truth: "I am fearfully and wonderfully made." (Psalm 139:14, NIV)

Lie: "I'm miserable, and nothing will change."

Truth: "The joy of the Lord is my strength." (Nehemiah 8:10, NIV)

Lie: "I feel all alone."

Truth: "My God is with me and will never leave me." ("I will never leave you nor forsake you." Hebrews 13:5, ESV)

Lie: "I'm a victim."

Truth: "I am more than a conqueror through Christ." (Romans 8:37, NIV)

CONCLUSION

You don't have to stay locked in a prison of lies. Jesus holds the keys to your freedom, and He is ready to set you free. Take every thought captive and make it obedient to Christ. Replace the lies with the truth of God's Word and watch as He transforms your mind and your life.

When we rely on the truth of God's Word, we can break free from the strongholds that have held us back. Let's start living in the freedom Jesus has already won for us!

_____

_____

_____

_____

_____

_____

_____

_____

_____

_____

_____

_____

_____

_____

TRUSTING WHEN WE DON'T UNDERSTAND

How Do I Trust God When I Don't Understand What He's Doing?

It's one of the toughest questions we face as Christians: *How do I trust God when I don't understand His plan?* When life seems confusing or painful, trusting God can feel like the hardest thing to do.

Proverbs 3:5-6 (NIV) gives us the answer, but living it out is certainly a challenge: "Trust in the Lord with all your heart and lean not on your own understanding; in all your ways submit to him, and he will make your paths straight."

It's easy to quote, but so difficult to live. Why? Because it's way easier to worry than to trust.

WHAT YOUR WORRIES REVEAL

Worry is something we all face, but here's a hard truth:

What you worry about the most often reveals where you trust God the least.

Think about that for a moment. When we worry, it's often because we're leaning on our own understanding rather than trusting in God's bigger plan.

Let's look at the story of Hannah. In her time, a woman's primary role in society was to bear children. Not having children was seen as a curse, and people believed it was a sign of God's disfavor.

Imagine the shame and pain Hannah felt, wondering if she had done something wrong or if God had abandoned her.
Year after year, it was the same. No children.

No answer to her prayers…BUT GOD

TRUSTING GOD IN THE TRIALS

Just like Hannah, you may be going through a season of waiting or trial. Maybe you're facing a difficult situation and starting to wonder if God is even listening.

But here's a key truth:

WE DON'T LEARN TO TRUST GOD IN THE GOOD TIMES; WE LEARN TO TRUST HIM IN THE TRIALS.

Hannah continued to trust God even when He seemed silent. She didn't turn away from God—she turned toward Him. Instead of shutting Him out, she poured out her heart in prayer.

CONCLUSION

Keep trusting. Just like Hannah, when you don't understand what God is doing, that's when you need to trust Him the most. Trusting God doesn't mean everything will suddenly make sense. It means you believe God is good, even when you don't see the full picture.

So, when you're tempted to worry, remember this:

Trust in the Lord with all your heart, even when you don't understand. God is working, even in the waiting, and He will make your paths straight in His perfect time.

GOD IS STILL IN CONTROL

Even When Everything Seems Out of Control, God Is Still in Control

Have you ever felt like life was spiraling out of control? Maybe things just didn't make sense, and you were wondering, "Where is God in all of this?"
Here's the truth: God is still in control.

It might not make sense right now, but God's got this. He hasn't left you, and He hasn't lost control.

GOD USES PAIN FOR PURPOSE

We serve a God who uses the pain we go through to accomplish His purpose. He turns our mess into a message and our tests into testimonies. What you're walking through today isn't wasted. God is working, even in the pain, to bring about something good.

Nothing has ever, or will ever, catch God by surprise. He knows what's going on, and He has a plan for it, even if you can't see it yet.

GIVE YOUR WORRIES TO GOD

The very thing you're worried about right now? God already knows. He cares deeply about it and has an answer. But here's the key: You have to *give it to Him*.

Whatever you hold on to, you carry. But if you cast your cares on Him, He promises to carry them for you.

1 Peter 5:7 (NIV) reminds us: "Cast all your anxiety on Him because He cares for you."

CONCLUSION

You are not alone. God's promise is that *He will never leave you or forsake you*. No matter how chaotic life feels, you are not alone.

Jesus also promised us peace—His peace. And because this peace doesn't come from the world, the world can't take it away.

So, as you face your struggles, remember this: God is still in control. Trust Him with your worries, cast your cares on Him, and receive His peace that passes all understanding.

WHY DID GOD ALLOW IT TO HAPPEN?

A Question Asked Since the Beginning of Time

This is one of the most difficult and profound questions people have asked since the beginning of time. When we face pain, loss, and suffering, it's natural to wonder why a loving and all-powerful God would allow it.

EVIL AND SUFFERING IN THE BIBLE

Contrary to what many believe, evil and suffering aren't contrary to the story of the Bible. In fact, evil and suffering are central to the story of the Bible. From the fall of humanity in Genesis to the suffering of Jesus on the cross, the Bible doesn't shy away from the reality of pain.

Christianity does something profound: it makes sense of, gives meaning to, and offers a solution for the evil and suffering we experience. No other worldview offers the hope, redemption, and ultimate victory over suffering that Christianity does.

IF GOD IS LOVING, WHY WOULD HE ALLOW SUFFERING?

One common question is, "If God is truly loving, why would He allow suffering?" The answer lies in the very nature of love itself.

IF LOVE IS A CHOICE, SUFFERING IS A POSSIBILITY.

The only way for love to be real is for it to be a choice. God gave us free will, the ability to choose between love and hate, between right and wrong.

But the freedom to choose good also brings with it the freedom to choose evil, and that's what makes evil and suffering possible.

WHY DID GOD GIVE US FREE WILL?

Why would God give us free will if it opens the door to evil and suffering? Because without free will, there can be no real love. God didn't want a relationship with robots or inanimate objects like rocks. He desired a relationship with people who could choose to love Him, and the only way for love to be genuine is for it to be freely chosen.

This freedom, however, also means we have the ability to choose evil—and when we do, sin enters the world. Sin leads to pain and suffering, not only for the one who sins but often for others as well.

THE CONSEQUENCE OF FREE WILL

When we choose evil, we choose sin, and sin leads to suffering. The brokenness we see in the world—wars, injustice, disease, and personal pain—is a result of humanity's misuse of free will.

If God were to remove all evil and suffering, He would either have to remove our freedom to choose, or He would have to remove us entirely. But God, in His love, allows us to continue choosing because He desires a genuine relationship with us, not one forced by control.

CONCLUSION

Suffering is painful and real, but it doesn't mean God is distant or unloving. The Bible tells the story of a God who entered into our suffering through Jesus Christ and provided a way out of it. God doesn't promise a life free of suffering, but He does promise to be with us through it and to ultimately bring an end to all suffering in His perfect timing. When you face pain, remember God's love gave you the freedom to choose, and His love offers you hope even in the midst of suffering.

WHO DO YOU THINK YOU ARE?
What You Think About You Matters

The way you answer this question can shape your entire life. Proverbs 23:7 (NKJV) says, "For as he thinks in his heart, so is he." In other words, your life will always move in the direction of your strongest thoughts.

GOD IS INTENTIONAL ABOUT WHO YOU ARE

All throughout Scripture, God is intentional and strategic in reminding us who we are in Him. He repeatedly tells us we are loved, chosen, forgiven, and redeemed. But why does God keep saying it over and over?

It's because there is often a gap between what God says about us and what we actually believe. This gap shapes how we live, and it often leads us to think and behave in ways that don't align with what God has already declared about us.

THE POWER OF YOUR THOUGHTS

The strength of your identity is revealed in the size of the problem it takes to discourage you. Think about the Israelites when they spied out the Promised Land. (Numbers 13) They saw themselves as grasshoppers compared to the giants, and their low self-perception kept them from stepping into what God had for them. Your life will reflect your thoughts, and if your thoughts are filled with fear or self-doubt, your actions will follow.

Your life is a mirror—it reflects how you think. Not just in your head, but in your heart. If your heart is filled with doubt or insecurity, it will flow into every area of your life—your work, your relationships, your decisions.

CONCLUSION

Align your thoughts with God's truth. Your life will follow your thinking, so God calls us to set our minds on things above. Philippians 4:8 (NIV) reminds us to think about *whatever is true, noble, right, pure, lovely, and admirable.*

God wants you to think about yourself the way He thinks about you, because when you believe what God says about you, you can start living like it.

So ask yourself, *Who do I think I am?* If your answer doesn't align with God's Word, then it's time to shift your thoughts. Believe what He says about you, and let your life reflect that truth!

_____

_____

_____

_____

_____

_____

_____

_____

_____

STEP OUT TO FIND OUT

You Have to Have Faith to Step Out in Obedience

The waters are getting ready to part in your life, but it's not going to look like it did last time.

Almost everyone has heard about the miraculous moment when the Red Sea parted, allowing the Israelites to cross over on dry ground. But there's another powerful moment in the Bible where God does something just as amazing—it just looks a little different.

In Joshua 3, the Israelites were about to enter the Promised Land, but once again they found themselves facing an obstacle—a body of water. This time, it wasn't the Red Sea, but the Jordan River.

A NEW GENERATION, A NEW WAY

This was a new generation, one that had heard stories of how God had parted the Red Sea for their ancestors. But now, things looked different. Joshua gave them a new instruction: When you see the Ark of the Covenant (a symbol of God's presence), follow it, and then you'll know which way to go.

It's crucial that we always let God's presence go before us and guide us. The first time God parted the waters, all Moses had to do was raise his staff, and the miracle happened right before the eyes of Israelites. But this time, there was a twist—God wasn't going to act until they moved first.

FAITH REQUIRES ACTION

The first time, God parted the sea, and then the Israelites moved. This time, the Israelites had to move, *then* God would part the waters.

Faith always requires action. Faith is not passive—it's active. It involves stepping out even when you don't know how things are going to turn out. Sometimes, God calls us to step into the unknown before He reveals what's next.

CONCLUSION

So, here's the question: Will you trust God even if this time your feet have to get wet first?

Maybe the miracle you're waiting for won't happen in the same way it did last time. Maybe you have to take that first step of faith before you see the waters part. God's ways aren't always predictable, but He's always faithful.

Step out in faith, and let God show you what He's going to do. He's ready to move in your life, but sometimes you have to take that first step to find out.

_____

_____

_____

_____

_____

_____

_____

_____

ELIMINATE TEMPTATION
You Are Not as Strong as You Think

Scripture: "So, if you think you are standing firm, be careful that you don't fall!"
(1 Corinthians 10:12, NIV)

RESTRAINT BIAS: THE OVERESTIMATION TRAP

Studies reveal that people drastically overestimate their ability to resist temptation, a concept known as "restraint bias." This bias leads us to believe we can handle more than we actually can. For example, imagine you're faced with a delicious piece of cake. You might confidently think, *I can resist this*. Yet, resisting temptation requires significant energy and willpower. The part of our brain that controls willpower wears out quickly, making us more vulnerable to giving in.

You fight the urge to yell at your coworkers all day long, but then you get home and blow up at our spouse. You white knuckle one thing and resist with all your might only to give in to the next thing. Self-control is a limited resource—the more we use it, the less we have. This is why overestimating our ability to resist temptation can be dangerous.

MOVE THE LINE

Let's consider the question "How close can I get to the line without sinning?" Often, we approach temptation by seeing how close we can get without crossing the line. But we wouldn't apply this logic in other critical areas of life.

Consider pilots. Would they ever calculate the least amount of fuel needed to barely reach their destination? Or would they ensure they have more than enough to arrive safely?

Instead of asking, "How close can I get?" we should ask, "How far can I stay?"

PUT DISTANCE BETWEEN YOU AND TEMPTATION

Why would you wait to resist a temptation in the future if you have the power to eliminate it today? Creating barriers between you and sin might seem restrictive, but in reality, it is freeing.

Psalm 16:6 says, "The boundary lines have fallen for me in pleasant places; surely I have a delightful inheritance." Boundaries are not about restriction but protection. They help us live a life free from the snares of sin.

Just because something is not inherently sinful doesn't mean it's beneficial. As Paul says, "'I have the right to do anything,' you might say—but not everything is beneficial. 'I have the right to do anything'—but not everything is constructive." (1 Corinthians 10:23) Wisdom calls us to discern not just what is permissible, but what is beneficial for our spiritual health.

_____

_____

_____

_____

_____

_____

CONCLUSION

Today, take a moment to reflect on the temptations you face. Are there areas where you overestimate your ability to resist? Are there boundaries you need to establish to protect your heart and mind? Remember, it's not about how close you can get to the line, but how far you can stay from it. Let God's wisdom guide you in setting those boundaries, ensuring they fall in pleasant places, leading you to a delightful inheritance.

GOD DOESN'T WANT YOU HAPPY?

What If I Told You God's Ultimate Priority Isn't Your Happiness?

Scripture: "But seek first his kingdom and his righteousness, and all these things will be given to you as well."
(Matthew 6:33, NIV)

THE PROBLEM WITH THE THEOLOGY OF HAPPINESS

The idea that "God wants you happy" sounds good, doesn't it? "Enjoy your life! Good things are in store for you!" But the problem with this theology of happiness is that it reduces God to a cosmic Coke machine. We start to believe God exists solely to serve us. When life doesn't go the way we want—when we aren't happy—we think God has failed us. Many people try religion, go to church, but when it doesn't lead to immediate happiness, they give up, thinking, *It didn't work.*

The truth is, your happiness isn't God's highest priority. While He delights in your joy, much like a parent does with their child, He desires something deeper. God doesn't want you to pursue happiness—He wants you to pursue Him. The goal isn't to seek God for the happiness He might provide, but to seek Him for who He is.

WHEN GOD DOESN'T WANT YOU HAPPY

1. GOD DOESN'T WANT YOU HAPPY WHEN IT LEADS TO SIN OR FOOLISHNESS

We often justify wrong choices because we think they will make us happy in the moment. But God cares more about your holiness than your temporary happiness. If happiness causes you to do something wrong or unwise, that's not the kind of happiness God wants for you.

2. GOD DOESN'T WANT YOU HAPPY WHEN IT'S BASED ON TEMPORARY THINGS

The happiness that comes from possessions, circumstances, or worldly success is fleeting. It's like building a house on sand—unstable and unreliable. God's desire is for you to find joy in things that are eternal, not just the temporary pleasures of this world.

GOD WANTS YOU BLESSED

God doesn't just want you to be happy in the superficial sense. He wants you to be blessed. The Greek word for blessed, *makarios*, means to be "supremely blessed, more than happy."

This blessing doesn't mean you'll never face difficulties, like sickness, job loss, or unexpected trials. It doesn't mean God will say yes to every prayer or give you everything you want. Instead, God's blessing is found in something far deeper—His presence in your life.

In the storms, God offers comfort. In your weakness, He gives strength. In trials, He provides joy. These blessings are far greater than the fleeting happiness the world offers.

YOU WEREN'T MADE FOR EARTH

Picture a fish on the beach. You could pile cash next to it, place it in a beach chair, and offer it a drink—but the fish would never be happy. Why? It wasn't designed for the beach. In the same way, you weren't made for earth. No matter how many moments of happiness you experience, they can't compare to what God has prepared for you in eternity.

Max Lucado said it best: "You weren't made for earth. Moments of happiness and joy cannot compare to what's ahead. Lower your expectations of earth. Not heaven. No new car, new wife, new baby, new boat will give you the joy your heart craves."

"Lower your expectations of earth." The things of this world—new cars, new homes, new relationships—will never satisfy the deepest longings of your heart. You were created for more than this world. True happiness and joy come from a relationship with God and the eternal hope we have in Him.

CONCLUSION

Today, reflect on where you've been seeking happiness. Have you reduced God to a cosmic vending machine? Are you chasing temporary pleasures instead of pursuing God Himself? Remember, God's desire is not just for your momentary happiness but for your eternal joy and blessing in Him. Seek first His kingdom and righteousness, and you will find the joy your heart craves.

PRAY THROUGH THE PAIN

If It's Big Enough to Worry About, It's Big Enough to Pray About!

Most of our biggest battles happen in our minds, where no one else can see. On the outside, we might look strong, but on the inside, we feel weak. We seem confident, but we're afraid. We show happiness on social media, but we're hurting. That's why we must learn to *pray through the pain.*

Philippians 4:4-7 (NIV)

"Rejoice in the Lord always. I will say it again: Rejoice! Let your gentleness be evident to all. The Lord is near. Do not be anxious about anything, but in every situation, by prayer and petition, with thanksgiving, present your requests to God. And the peace of God, which transcends all understanding, will guard your hearts and your minds in Christ Jesus."

Paul wrote these words from prison, awaiting trial, and yet he urges us to rejoice and pray in every situation—especially when we feel anxious.

Is it a sin to feel anxious? No.

Even Jesus prayed through His anxiety in the Garden of Gethsemane. Anxiety itself isn't a sin, but it's an invitation to pray.

WHAT DOES PAUL MEAN BY "DO NOT BE ANXIOUS ABOUT ANYTHING"?

He's not saying we'll never feel anxiety, but he's urging us to take every anxious thought to God. He reminds us that in every situation, we should pray.

IF IT'S ON YOUR MIND, IT'S ON GOD'S HEART.

- Worried about a doctor's appointment? **Pray!**
- Facing a tough decision? **Pray!**
- Anxious about going back to school or work? **Pray!**

CONCLUSION

Present your requests to God. Paul says, "Let your needs be known" to God. Don't hold anything back. When you bring your pain, worry, and fear to Him, you open the door for His peace to guard your heart and mind in Christ.

When life feels overwhelming, don't carry it alone—pray through the pain, and let God bring you the peace that surpasses all understanding.

_____

_____

_____

_____

_____

_____

WHY SHOULD WE TRUST WHAT THE BIBLE HAS TO SAY?

Don't Believe Everything You Read

Ain't that the truth? Just because something is in print doesn't make it true. So why should we trust what the Bible says?

1. THE BIBLE TELLS US ABOUT REAL PEOPLE AND REAL EVENTS

Unlike other ancient writings filled with myths and legends, the Bible describes real people and real events. It doesn't sugarcoat life or try to tell fanciful stories. These are things that actually happened. The Bible doesn't read like fiction because it's rooted in historical reality.

2. THE BIBLE WAS WRITTEN BY EYEWITNESSES

Another reason we can trust the Bible is that it was written by people who witnessed the events they recorded. They didn't invent stories; they were simply writing down what they had seen so future generations would know the truth.

Peter even writes, "We did not follow cleverly invented stories, but we were eyewitnesses."
(2 Peter 1:16, NIV)

3. THE BIBLE POINTS US TO THE MOST IMPORTANT EVENT IN HISTORY

Most importantly, the Bible points us to Jesus Christ—His life, death, and resurrection. This is the central event of human history, and through the Bible, we are introduced to the living Word—Jesus Himself.

The Bible is no ordinary book. It was written over 1,500 years by more than forty different authors in three different languages, yet it presents one unified message:
God's plan to redeem a fallen world through Jesus Christ.

CONCLUSION

The Bible is also incredibly practical. It deals honestly with human sin, weakness, and brokenness. Life is presented as it really is, and through every story, we see the reality of God's love and grace.

The truth within its pages isn't just theological—it's life-changing. As General Robert E. Lee once observed, "The Bible is a book in comparison with which all others in my eyes are of minor importance, and which in all my complexities and distresses has never failed to give me light and strength."

In the pages of the Bible, you'll find the light and strength you need for today and every day. It's not just a book; it's God's Word, alive and speaking to us in every situation. Trust it because it points you to the ultimate truth—Jesus Christ.

_____

_____

_____

_____

_____

_____

STOP COMPARING YOUR CALLING

The Fastest Way to Kill Something Special Is to Compare It to Something Else

Have you ever found yourself looking at someone else's life and thinking, *I wish I could do that?* It's so easy to compare our lives, our abilities, and even our callings to those of others. But the fastest way to kill something special is to compare it to something else.

The reason you can't do what someone else does is simple: *You weren't called to their purpose.*

1. YOU ARE PERFECTLY CREATED BY GOD TO FULFILL HIS PURPOSE FOR YOU

Ephesians 2:10 (NLT) says:

"For we are God's masterpiece. He has created us anew in Christ Jesus, so we can do the good things he planned for us long ago."

Think about that for a moment. You are God's masterpiece—uniquely designed, gifted, and called to fulfill His purpose for you, not someone else's. Everything God creates, He creates with a specific purpose, and that includes you.

Your birth is evidence that your purpose is necessary. There is no substitute for you. No one else can fulfill the calling God has placed on your life. So, why would we waste time comparing ourselves to others when we are uniquely designed for a different mission?

You are created by God, for God. So, do everything for His glory, not for the approval of others. We often get caught up in trying to impress people, living for the approval of the crowd. But who are we really trying to impress? Who is *"they"*?

COMPARISON IS THE ENEMY OF CALLING

2. YOU CAN'T FULFILL GOD'S PURPOSE FOR YOU WHILE COMPARING YOURSELF TO SOMEONE ELSE

When you start comparing your calling to someone else's, you lose focus. You can't run your race if you're constantly looking at someone else's lane.

Hebrews 12:1-2 (NIV) gives us this powerful reminder:

"And let us run with perseverance the race marked out for us, fixing our eyes on Jesus, the pioneer and perfecter of faith."

There's a race marked out for you, but you can't run it if you're too busy comparing your pace, your gifts, or your calling to someone else's. Fix your eyes on Jesus—the author and perfecter of your faith. When you do, you'll realize it's impossible to win someone else's race.

God has given each of us our own unique path to walk and our own race to run. We need to focus on *our* calling and stop looking sideways.

_____

_____

_____

_____

_____

CONCLUSION

The fastest way to kill something special is to compare it. You are God's masterpiece, created for a specific purpose. Don't let comparison rob you of your calling. Fix your eyes on Jesus, run the race marked out for you, and fulfill the special purpose only you can accomplish.

HAPPY MEAL

We Are Created for Heaven, So Stop Living for This World

As a kid, one of my favorite things was going to Burger King, but not for the reason you might think. It wasn't about the food—it was about the Happy Meal. Actually, I didn't even like McDonald's food all that much, but their Happy Meal toys? They were the real deal!

I remember the anticipation of reaching into that bag, excited to see the toy inside. But more often than not, after a few minutes of excitement, the disappointment would set in.

The toys always failed to deliver:

- Cheap plastic.
- Never worked the way they were supposed to.
- Usually got thrown on the floor within a few minutes.
- Nowadays, you even have to put them together!

No child on the planet has ever received lasting happiness from a Happy Meal. The problem with a Happy Meal is that the "happy" wears off—it never sticks around for long.

THE HAPPINESS FADES, BUT THE HUNGER STAYS

You know what? I'm no different than my son. The only difference between his Happy Meals and mine is that my "Happy Meals" are a bit more expensive—a new car, a house, a new gadget, or something else I thought would bring lasting happiness.

But here's the thing: Every time I try to buy happiness, the happiness fades. The initial thrill might last a moment, but sooner or later the joy fades and the hunger for something more stays.

THE HAPPINESS GOES AWAY, BUT THE HUNGER STAYS

I know I'm not alone in that feeling. Many of us are looking for happiness in things that can't deliver—searching for joy in all the wrong places.

SEARCHING FOR SOMETHING THIS WORLD CAN'T PROVIDE

The reason the hunger stays is that we are searching in this world for something that only heaven can provide.

God created us for *more than this world*. The temporary pleasures and joys we find here, no matter how exciting, will always leave us feeling empty at the end. The thrill fades, and we're left hungry for something deeper. That's because *our souls were created for eternity, not for the fleeting pleasures of this world.*

HEAVEN IS WHERE THE HUNGER GOES AWAY AND THE HAPPINESS STAYS

In heaven, that longing and hunger we feel deep inside will finally be satisfied. The Bible promises us that in heaven, there will be no more sorrow, no more pain, and no more hunger. The joy we will experience in God's presence will never fade or disappoint.

_____

_____

_____

_____

Revelation 21:4 (NIV) says:

"He will wipe every tear from their eyes. There will be no more death or mourning or crying or pain, for the old order of things has passed away."

CONCLUSION

We were created for heaven, not for this world. The happiness we seek here is fleeting, but in heaven, the happiness stays, and the hunger is gone forever. So, stop searching for happiness in the things of this world and fix your eyes on the joy that will never fade—the joy of eternity with Jesus.

Let's live for *heaven,* where the joy is eternal and the hunger is finally satisfied!

_____

_____

_____

_____

_____

_____

_____

_____

_____

_____

PRUNING IS NOT PUNISHMENT
In Life You Will Get Cut

Have You Ever Felt Like You're Being "Cut Back" in Life—Facing Challenges, Setbacks, or Painful Circumstances?

Here's an important truth: Pruning is not punishment. It's part of God's loving process of making you even more fruitful.

In John 15:1-2 (NIV), Jesus says:

"I am the true vine, and my Father is the gardener. He cuts off every branch in me that bears no fruit, while every branch that does bear fruit He prunes so that it will be even more fruitful."

PRUNING VS. PUNISHMENT

At first glance, *pruning* and *punishment* can seem very similar. Both involve pain, and both feel like something is being taken away. But the intention behind them is drastically different.

Pruning is God's reward to you for having something of value within you. It's a sign that you're already producing fruit, and He wants to take you to the next level. He wouldn't prune you if you were a dying bush. He sees your potential and knows that by cutting away the dead ends, you will become even more fruitful.

God isn't punishing you when you go through difficult times. Instead, He's shaping and refining you for greater things.

SETBACKS ARE OFTEN SETUPS FOR A COMEBACK

What may feel like a setback right now could very well be a setup for a comeback. God is working behind the scenes, preparing you for the next season of fruitfulness.

Romans 8:32 (NIV) reminds us:

If God would not spare His own Son, why not you? If even Jesus, the perfect Son of God, was pruned and went through suffering, we shouldn't be surprised when we face difficulties. It's all part of God's process of shaping us into His likeness.

CONCLUSION

God often calls us out and away from our comfort. We cannot be comfortable and Christlike at the same time. If we want to grow in Christlikeness, God will always call us out of our comfort zones.

Pruning, though painful, is a sign that God is at work in your life. He's preparing you for more— more fruitfulness, more impact, more growth. So the next time you feel the cuts, remember: *pruning isn't punishment—it's preparation.* Trust the process, stay connected to the vine, and watch how God brings forth new life from your season of pruning.

_____

_____

_____

_____

_____

AUTHORITY

If You Are in Christ, You Have Miraculous Authority over Darkness in the Name of Jesus

In Matthew 10:1 (NIV), we see this clearly:

> Jesus called his twelve disciples to him and gave them authority to drive out impure spirits and to heal every disease and sickness.

This authority is not our own—it comes from Christ. Think of a police officer. A police officer doesn't have the *power* to make a car stop by their own strength, but they have *authority*—the weight of the law behind them. In the same way, God is a miraculous God, who gives us authority over darkness in the name of Jesus!

FIGHTING WITH CHRIST'S POWER

We are not fighting spiritual battles with our own power. We are fighting with Christ's power. The enemy's mission is clear—he wants to steal, kill, and destroy. (John 10:10) But Jesus has already defeated him!

A few key points to remember:

- Don't assume every problem is the result of demonic influence.
- But also, don't assume any problem isn't.

When Jesus rose from the dead, He defeated darkness once and for all. This victory means that, through Him, we have authority over the forces of darkness.

DARKNESS AND LIGHT

Here's something important to understand: Darkness is not the opposite of light. It is the *absence* of light. Jesus said, "I am the light of the world" (John 8:12, ESV), and He dwells within each of us as believers. This means that whenever there is spiritual darkness, when you walk in, light walks in.

Next time you face spiritual darkness, say it with confidence:

> "I take authority over this darkness
> in the name of Jesus."

CONCLUSION

We have victory in Jesus. Remember, greater is the one who is in you than the one who is in the world.
(1 John 4:4) You're not fighting *for* victory, you are fighting *from* victory! Jesus has already overcome, and He has given you the authority to stand firm and shine His light in a dark world.

Walk in that authority today.

_____

_____

_____

_____

_____

_____

_____

_____

GOD IS WITH YOU

You Are Not Alone, God Is with You

No matter what you're facing right now, you are not alone. God is with you.

In Matthew's account of Jesus's birth, he shares a powerful truth with a Jewish audience eagerly awaiting their Messiah. Rather than focus on the manger scene, Matthew emphasizes the purpose and identity of Jesus:

"'She will give birth to a son, and you are to give him the name Jesus, because he will save his people from their sins … The virgin will conceive and give birth to a son, and they will call him Immanuel.'"
(*God with us*). —Matthew 1:21, 23 (NIV)

EMMANUEL—GOD WITH US

That name, Emmanuel, is packed with meaning. For centuries, God's people had been waiting for this promise, prophesied by Isaiah 740 years earlier: "The virgin will conceive and give birth to a son, and will call him Immanuel." (Isaiah 7:14, NIV) And finally, He was here—**God with us!**

Jesus wasn't just a distant, uninvolved deity. He wasn't watching from afar. Instead, the Word became flesh. (John 1:14) He came close. God Himself entered into the mess of our lives to walk with us, to save us, and to comfort us.

GOD IS WITH YOU RIGHT NOW

That promise wasn't just for then—it's for *you* today.

- *Feeling alone?* God is with you as your companion.
- *Sick?* God is with you as your healer.
- *Lost?* God is with you as your guide.
- *Hurting?* God is with you as your hope.
- *Weak?* God is with you as your strength.
- *Struggling with sin?* God is with you as your Savior.

In whatever circumstances you find yourself, the God of all comfort is with you and beside you. You don't have to carry your burdens alone. The One who created the universe cares deeply about you and has chosen to walk through this life with you.

CONCLUSION

God is not distant or detached. He is Emmanuel—God with us. So no matter what you are going through today, remember He is near. He is with you in the valleys and on the mountaintops, in your struggles and in your victories.
Rest in that truth:

God is with you.

_____
_____
_____
_____
_____
_____

THE POWER TO CHANGE
Why Do You Do What You Do?

Think about this question: *Why do you do what you do?* The truth is, you do what you do because of what you think of yourself.

The way we perceive ourselves drives our actions and behaviors.

The Bible says in Proverbs 23:7 (NKJV):

"For as he thinks in his heart, so is he."

In other words, if you want to change what you do, you must first change what you think of you.

WHY DO WE BELIEVE THE NEGATIVE MORE THAN THE POSITIVE?

Isn't it interesting that it's often easier to believe the negative things about ourselves than the positive? Have you ever wondered why that is? *The devil is a liar*, and he's been lying to you since the day you were born.

He constantly whispers lies about who you aren't, what you can't do, and why you'll never be good enough. We hear these toxic lies so often that we start to believe them. But Jesus said, "the truth will set you free." (John 8:32, ESV) If we hold on to God's truth about us, we can break free from these chains.

THE DEVIL ATTACKS YOUR IDENTITY, NOT JUST YOUR ACTIONS

When you make a mistake or do something wrong, notice how the enemy doesn't just accuse you of *doing* something bad. He goes further—he attacks your identity.

He tries to convince you that you are bad, you'll never change, and you're hopeless.

The devil's lie is: "You can't change; it's just the way you are!"

THE CYCLE OF DESTRUCTION: DISTORTED IDENTITY

What happens when we believe these lies? Our *distorted identity* begins to sabotage our success. This distorted view of ourselves leads to destructive habits, and those habits only reinforce our distorted identity. It's a vicious cycle:

1. **Your distorted identity** sabotages your success.
2. **Your destructive habits** reinforce your distorted identity.

You may think, *I'm just not disciplined,* or *I've always been this way.* But that's not who God says you are!

THE POWER OF A CHRIST-CENTERED IDENTITY

The good news is that when you embrace a *Christ-centered identity*, everything changes. When you start to see yourself as God sees you, your habits begin to change. And those *Christ-honoring habits* reinforce your Christ-centered identity. It's a powerful cycle of transformation:

1. **A Christ-centered identity** leads to Christ-honoring habits.

2. **Christ-honoring habits** reinforce a Christ-centered identity.

This is the power to change.

FOCUS ON WHO YOU WANT TO BECOME

So, instead of focusing on *what* you want to do, start by deciding *who* you want to become. *Who has God called you to be?* When your identity is rooted in Christ, everything else will follow.

CONCLUSION

You aren't defined by your past. You aren't limited by your mistakes. You are *who God says you are*—and through Christ, you have the power to change.

Let go of the lies, hold on to the truth, and start living in the freedom and power of your true identity in Christ!

_____

_____

_____

_____

_____

_____

_____

_____

_____

_____

_____

STRENGTHEN WITH POWER
General Prayers Don't Move God to Specific Actions

We know we should pray, but sometimes it's hard. We get bored, distracted, or even feel guilty for not praying enough. Often, when we do pray, our prayers can be too vague or small, and we might wonder why we aren't seeing more of God's power in our lives.

TWO BIG PRAYER MISTAKES:
- Our prayers are often too small.
- Our prayers are too general.
(God, be with me today.)

But God wants us to pray *boldly* and *specifically* because He is able to do far more than we could ever ask or imagine. My prayer for you today is the same as Paul's prayer to the church in Ephesus:

Ephesians 3:16-17 (NIV)

"I pray that out of His glorious riches He may strengthen you with power through His Spirit in your inner being, so that Christ may dwell in your hearts through faith."

Paul didn't pray for God to simply "be with them." He prayed for power—power to stand strong, to overcome temptation, to be bold in faith, and to experience God's presence deeply. That's the kind of prayer that moves mountains!

PRAY FOR POWER:

- *Power to forgive* when it's hard.
- *Power to remain calm* when life is chaotic.
- *Power to be confident* when doubts creep in.
- *Power to experience peace* even in the middle of trials.
- *Power to speak with wisdom and faith* when you don't know what to say.

CONCLUSION

God is able to give you more than you can ask or even imagine!

Ephesians 3:20-21 (NIV)

"Now to Him who is able to do immeasurably more than all we ask or imagine, according to His power that is at work within us, to Him be glory in the church and in Christ Jesus throughout all generations, for ever and ever! Amen."

God's power is at work in you, not just to get by, but to thrive in faith. He is able to do *immeasurably more* than what you are asking for today. So, pray specifically, pray boldly, and trust that God will strengthen you with power through His Spirit!

_____

_____

_____

_____

_____

_____

NO MORE _____
Jesus Is Coming Back Soon!

I've always been fascinated by heaven—the thought of it, the talk of it. One of the reasons is because of how the Bible describes it.

Often, the most effective way to describe something isn't to say what it *is*, but to say what it *isn't*. At the very end of the Bible, the apostle John tells us about heaven by describing what *won't* be there. In Revelation 21, he uses this powerful phrase:

"No more _____."

Let's take a look at what won't be in heaven, according to John.

1. NO MORE DEATH

In heaven, there will be no more death—not momentarily, but forever.

I know that with everything going on in our world, death can feel like a heavy subject we'd rather avoid. It's uncomfortable, and we don't know when or how it will come. But here's the thing: We have an enemy who loves to use the reality of death to bully and intimidate us. Yet in heaven, that fear is gone. Death is defeated—forever.

2. NO MORE DARKNESS

In heaven, there will be no more darkness. John tells us that God Himself will be our light. There will be no more fear of the unknown, no more confusion or uncertainty. His presence will fill everything with light, and nothing will be hidden.

3. NO MORE DISORDER

Imagine a place with no more disorder. No more chaos, no more confusion. Our world is filled with brokenness and disarray, but in heaven, everything will be perfectly ordered according to God's will. It will be a place of perfect peace and harmony.

CONCLUSION

Every day, we are one step closer to that glorious reality. As we live in a world filled with death, darkness, and disorder, our hearts should long even more for Jesus's return.

The day is coming when everything will be made new. We wait with joyful anticipation for that moment when He will wipe every tear from our eyes, and the Spirit and the bride say, "Come."

Are you ready for His return? The promise of heaven is not just a distant hope—it's a living reality that should stir us to long deeper and wait eagerly for the day when Jesus will come again.

_____

_____

_____

_____

_____

_____

ABOUT THE AUTHOR

Kevin Eloy is the founder and senior pastor of *theCause Church* in Hyannis, MA, a community passionate about pursuing the presence of God. He is also the founder of The Disciplined Dad, a movement dedicated to helping men grow in faith, leadership, fitness, and family life. His mission is to help both men and women become wholehearted followers of Jesus, equipping them to live with discipline and purpose in every area of life.

Kevin was born and raised on Cape Cod, MA, where he and his wife, Susan, live with their son, Beauman Grey (Beau), and their golden doodle, Penny. When he's not preaching, coaching, or creating content, he enjoys training in CrossFit, listening to music, and watching mixed martial arts.

Follow Kevin on all socials and be sure to subscribe to his YouTube channel where you can find short daily devotionals every weekday morning.

YouTube: https://www.youtube.com/@IamKevinEloy

Facebook:
https://www.facebook.com/kevin.f.eloy

Instagram:
https://www.instagram.com/iamkevineloy/

TikTok:
https://www.tiktok.com/@kevin.eloy86

https://www.kevineloy.com/

www.ingramcontent.com/pod-product-compliance
Lightning Source LLC
Chambersburg PA
CBHW020243010526
44107CB00002B/77